A Little Thought Book
88 Keys of Consciousness

Al Rush

Professional Misfits, Inc.
www.professionalmisfits.com

COPYRIGHT NOTICE

All Rights Reserved

© 2012 Professional Misfits, Inc.
Published by Professional Misfits, Inc., Chicago, Illinois

First Printing - Hardcopy December, 2012

Written by Al Rush
Edited by Harvey Ostreicher, Al Rush, Gary Rush, Milagros Rush, Sean Rush
Cover illustration by Al Rush, Sean Rush
Book design and layout by Al Rush, Sean Rush

ISBN 978-0-9795799-9-8

All rights reserved. No part of this book, either in part or in whole, may be reproduced, transmitted or utilized in any form or by any means, electronic or mechanical, including photocopying or any other means of photographic reproduction, recording, or by any information storage and retrieval system, without the prior written permission from the publisher, Professional Misfits, Inc., except for brief quotations embodied in critical reviews and articles.

www.professionalmisfits.com

Dedication

To my parents, who cared for me in times light and dark.

To little bro, may all his dreams come true.

To my friend Harvey, because he seeks the best in everything.

To the collective of many peoples, whose lives have taught me much.

To the Ancient of days, for whom I place my faith.

A Little Thought Book
88 Keys of Consciousness

Prelude

Overture ....
Thought from the Author ....

    Interlude - *A message from Atlantis* ....   1 | 01
        Act 1 - **AVALA**

    Interlude - *The key of conscious tranquility* ....   2 | 07
        Act 2 - **PETEH**

    Interlude - *An adversary is the reflection of* ....   3 | 19
        Act 3 - **AAGAN**

    Interlude - *An artist is unique who may be* ....   4 | 37
        Act 4 - **AHWEI**

    Interlude - *The tradition of* ....   5 | 44
        Act 5 - **NAAMI**

    Interlude - *The unity of people brings* ....   6 | 54
        Act 6 - **LASAM**

    Interlude - *Hands of freedom end* ....   7 | 73
        Act 7 - **VONIS**

Index ....
About the Author ....
About Professional Misfits, Inc. ....

A Little Thought Book
88 Keys of Consciousness

Overture

Let me first start by stating the obvious, I am not a prophet; neither am I anything special separate from other people. An idealist, perhaps....... An observer, more than likely, but in the end, I am no more than this.

I write.

To translate life perceived is perhaps the best way to describe who I am. If anything, this book serves as an extension of my journals to kindle the kingdom around us.

Charged with that understanding, it is my pleasure to introduce the 88 Keys of Consciousness, a philosophy of symbology that I have come to cherish from the journey of its making. It is not for the wealth of wisdom contained in its pages, and it is not for its rich symbolism of unique language sparked from the wellspring of imagination. But more-so, it is for those moments where inspiration struck in the most unlikely of times and places.

I have written amongst the rich, I have edited amongst the poor. I have written when time was on my side, I have written in defiance against no time. I have kept passages on my computer, on paper from the fine parchment of journals to shreds of napkins and Post-it® notes. In essence, this undertaking was forged from tattered collages of scraps, and the greatest reward is when everything came together into the complete work now presented before you.

A Little Thought Book - simple in appearance, profound in its intent with hopes of prospering on its own, even well beyond my time. It is my dream to have something special for everyone and if even one of these words manages to kindle the soul of any reader, then every experience, every trial, and every joy spent to bring the 88 Keys of Consciousness to life would have all been worth it a thousandfold.

Al Rush

Thought from the Author

"My words can be stranger than fiction, yet nothing is what it seems. Read, enjoy, reflect, and apply what is learned, for what is gained in mind builds the sure foundation for insight that books alone cannot hope to touch."

Al Rush

A Little Thought Book
88 Keys of Consciousness

AVALA

A message from Atlantis gives choice and change to the kingdom of our world.

Act 1

MESSAGE

That which created all things from the beginning shall return and reclaim the end to redeem a new beginning.

The Ancient of days, that humanity has long since sought, shall heal the breach that has worked to separate us from our Creator.

It is not easy for us to accept the origin when the origin itself is hidden beyond our flesh, and understand that everything we hold dear contains a perfect order to be fruitful, multiply, and hold sovereignty with all the earth.

Such a decree came with a promise that in the end of time, our reward in spirit is to be redeemed with heaven's grace forever.

AVALA

The message was sent, many have heard of it, only few care for it.

Beyond earthly achievements, time moves and perception is quickened by our willingness to behold creation's plan unfold before our very eyes.

It is in faith that must be kept, for we who stand shall be charged to pierce the moment of grace for all to enter therein.

"The message sent is heard by we who stand."

ATLANTIS

Atlantis....... A divided remembrance before the great flood of antiquity, where lands were younger and its people learned.

Two bloodlines contended against each other for dominion; the first cursed, the second blessed, with the first becoming mightier than the second.

Atlantis then rose to power, only to fall when the mighty serpent of the air was glorified, leading to the days where chaos foamed, the waves crashed, and whole lands perished beneath the rain while its kingdom ceased.

The tempest of a divine fist changed the face of Atlantis in that single moment, and most who remained were quick to neglect the past held close within them.

AVALA

After that time, generations passed by with only fragments preserved to reshape our lands into the vast kingdoms we know today.

Mark the signs and keep watch, for what happened before ended in betrayal, yet what will come to pass shall reclaim our legacy.

"Prepare yourself for when Atlantis rises, change will come."

CHOICE

Choice is like a fork of a flowing river, made to determine and develop individuality for each progression of growth and experience.

It is within choice that, which can spark a conflict and is, at times, condemned if choice is against the established laws of any given kingdom.

One's freedom of choice may be against all that is acceptable, even if choice in itself is like a fountain overflowing without any measure of limit.

AVALA

Nevertheless, the right to choose cannot be undone and can only grow stronger, even in times when tyranny abounds.

"In every choice, choose wisely."

CHANGE

Change is a constant, for nothing stagnates except the awareness that everything shifts with each passing moment.

Enjoy the moment for what it can give, and linger not to relive the exact moment nor seek to reproduce its exact feeling, for the nature of change is like whispers in the wind that gently blow the fallen leaves from one place to the other.

One moment, friends are brought together while the next scatters everyone abroad to their own fate of choosing; a gathering is held, a time shared, only to move into something new.

Identical experiences are never held twice as many might try.

AVALA

When attempted, something will always be different for better or worse, and never the same.

Change will not allow it, for all actions are bound to its function.

"Be content to accept change, as each moment shall never be again."

KINGDOM

An earthly kingdom is prosperous when principles are set forth to preserve and defend the general welfare of its subjects.

Many may not readily know this, but a kingdom's foundation is built on the faithful support of its subjects, and a kingdom can easily collapse if a kingdom's subjects are not properly cared for or fealty is broken between subject and king.

Education for wisdom guiding the way, conscious health and nutrition hallowed in our young, abundance of wealth distributed evenly to give fair opportunity to advance, and social zeal for common defense, are pivotal in the sustaining of a prosperous kingdom.

AVALA

If any of these are lacking, the kingdom becomes lacking.

If any of these fall, the kingdom falls.

"When all subjects are kept in prosperity, a kingdom endures the test of time."

WORLD

Our world lives, did you not know?

In the wake of forgotten truth, memories are never lost should records be burnt by a tyrant's hand.

Our world is older, shining as a bearer of life that ultimately becomes a temple of heavenly fire, in its promised time, to make all things new of radiant splendor.

The spirit of restoration has taken root; the fiery steps for a glorious eternity are set in motion.

AVALA

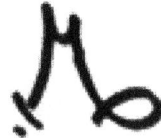

Flesh will not survive the times to come, for where spirit is, flesh is not and where flesh is, spirit is not.

Take heed to yourselves, for the world's end will try many to be counted worthy to receive the elixir of life, beyond our world.

"A world that lives for us shall not be ignored."

PETEH

The key of conscious tranquility gives future insight to a network of time, symbol, magic, and creation with a dream to infinity.

Act 2

KEY

At times, we are born to live against ourselves, prisoners to be lost in chains of iron that bind into a mortal coil of servitude.

Without seeing, we look to walk within a dimly lit maze of earthly splendor; like a maze of fractured mirrors where the exit is clearly witnessed beyond the blur of reflections, yet with little hope to reach without the guide who holds the key.

We search for every answer except for what the Ancient of days gives freely.

A gift from above to partake with respect for the faithful, a living testament to become the trusted guide whose key points the way out for the conscious heart.

PETEH

Seek that which is blessed, ordained from sacred sources, for life is like a child's playground mixed within a tempest of swirling chaos, and we are forever changed for the best, when the key is revealed.

"The exit above requires the key to step in."

CONSCIOUS

From the beginning, a movement of time accelerates to build experience on itself into the conscious mind where its end is the essence of all things learned before.

Experience gained contributes to our conscious sea, by which we increase in awareness collectively with each passing moment.

In life, we look to something new, and time is precious, funneling our growth towards the end while we yet breathe.

What is preached of our fall is the consequence of separation, a separation from divine intention by the lives we live and choices we make.

However, something remarkable is within reach; creation begins perfectly and shall end no less perfectly.

When the appointed hour is crossed, a conscious revival shall be kindled to spread unconditionally to all kingdoms before the end of time.

This is who we are, this is where we're headed, and everything living in all times shall be thanked for it..

"By the hand of all, our conscious sea moves to be set free."

TRANQUILITY

The mind is in constant flux.

Many are trained to think this way, with thoughts racing, fluttering, and dancing like cascading waterfalls without end.

That is one's illusion; the flux can end and from its end begins tranquility, where all thoughts cease.

It is found in the most unlikely of places, within, a oneness only experienced as calm without measure, a spiritual alignment.

Close off all external sounds and lie still.

The loudest sounds will bubble and surface, ride the mind until the last thought fades, and there will the journey begin.

"One's tranquility is breath from within."

FUTURE

The wise of days past advised us to live for the present and only do what the extent of that day requires with little concern for tomorrow.

Everything has its proper place and time, determined by one's actions in the present, based on all records of the past in remembrance.

Yet, the future is not known.

All efforts made by earthly kingdoms to exact the future end in vain.

Truly, we attempt to predict using formulas, projected forecasts, and analysis from streams of data with schedules set to claim that upon such and such time, it shall be done accordingly.

Yet, the future is not known, for the future is clever enough to hide within threads of variability.

Variables of choice negate predestination because in theory, if the future could be perfected simply by predictions, then our personal journeys would be rendered absolutely meaningless as we would be nothing more than motion without consciousness, fulfilling someone's predetermined end.

We must be clever when measuring the cup of existence, as predictions of the future only serve to reveal a chance into what may or may not be.

Like painting to a fresh canvas, we make our own lives in the now.

"By living for today, the future becomes reality."

INSIGHT

To speak, concerning affairs governing politics, is frowned by many, believing it better not to discuss openly more-so than to speak truly and suffer conflict of personal bias.

However, there is a key difference between bias governing over the fact of a matter and the fact itself.

Discard the ego of personal bias and the fact remains.

Understand that politics discussed is essential to check corruption from overstepping into tyranny.

The need to inform must be encouraged and not stifled because factual information for its own sake can enlighten many away from lies.

We are fortunate to live in a time where information is networked freely, but all it takes is a calculated power play to steal all we possess and what would seem to be taken for granted today may become a rare commodity tomorrow.

Share the facts, stay informed, and keep watch to know that, which potentially can affect us all.

"Sharing insight is our best defense."

NETWORK

Contrary to popular belief, earthly kingdoms have shared within themselves an underlined system of communication.

At the surface, what appears to be an outward conflict between kingdoms for coveting land, resources, and wealth, actually promotes war, only to further a secret union.

Traditions, dogma, and politics give the external appearance of independence, but there is a subtle language, a clever network exchanged to the point of ignorance.

Currency, or simpler - *numbers*, have kept relations between kingdoms closer than words ever could and stands as a unified language, bringing generations together to promote a synthesis of symbiosis.

PETEH

This network is powerful and feared, traveling the lengths of the earth to give or take as it pleases.

Kings are raised and lowered by its web and ties are made or broken by they, who have more, demanding of they, who have less, but without the network's influence when it was needed - visions for a kingdom's future would be in vain.

"Between earthly kingdoms, the network speaks."

TIME

The idea of measured time resides within one's personal acceptance of social consensus.

However, just as pure smoke moves fluidly through space with neither form nor substance, so will time act to stretch beyond consensus by being a radical agent that quickens itself from the experiences we impose upon it.

As a result, we indirectly influence humanity's promise of growth through fluctuations in time's perpetual quickening.

And when the zenith is breached, then shall there exist a timeless moment that intersects all points, a radical tempest neither static nor constant.

Thus, an hour can be like a minute, and a minute an eternity.

Dispel the veil of measurement and a glorious life awaits those willing to travel, where time becomes pliable like fresh potter's clay.

"There is no time like the best of time."

SYMBOL

A dogma of reality is the belief in symbols.

Truly, the power of belief is influenced by symbols reflected from within one's soul at any given time.

Let it be known that symbols, whether scribed or painted as language, spoken aloud or reflected in silence, hold profound effects in the way our reality is shaped by how our minds are shaped.

We create, that is what we do, and symbols assist to manifest that creation.

PETEH

This revelation should remind us to personally uphold responsibility whenever symbols are brought forth upon the earth; for every symbol can be a blessing or an entropy to all kingdoms unaware.

"A symbol crafted is a charmed affect."

MAGIC

Magic is mystical to people unawares, a schooled mystery whose knowledge enchants even the secret arrows of society.

The schism, to command forces swirls fiercely within many, long since the younger days of creation.

It is a subject not easy to keep clear from, since magic is clearly evident and abundantly well hidden in badges, crests, logos, seals, symbols, tattoos, and words throughout recorded history.

But know this, when the idea behind magic is identified and understood, the mystical aspect fades away to reveal a methodology - an order from the midst of chaos.

A science is born, methodical, predictable, provable, and repeatable.

However, if this understanding is absent to anyone who witnesses this, then they shall be quick to coin the experience as magic without thinking it through.

"Magic is that which is not understood."

CREATION

There is only creation, having no opposite while standing on its own accord.

It is a popular belief that without destruction, creation can never be.

However, the contention for destruction is an illusion, for there is no destruction, only the creation of destruction.

This fragment of truth is essential for growth of the conscious soul, to recognize that we create within the constraints of perceived reality.

Creation itself is like a singularity of refined spiritual foundations, the finger that bestows life from within which inspires the will of all thought, motive, and action.

A single light can create possibility; it is the one constant that moves spirit beyond flesh.

We create in likeness, it's what we do best, and creation is readily available to anyone that willingly accepts who we are and the reality we assist by creation.

"Envisioned light marks the sketch of creation."

DREAM

There is a vast possibility in the land of dreams, but a dreamer's neglect for remembrance helps to push dreams further into a hazy morning of forgetfulness.

In slumber, fantastic wonders kindle the imagination without doors, locks, or keys and when dreaming, the only rules existing are self imposed, for there are no rules.

Anything is possible in a dream....... *Anything*.

There is little logic involved on our own and should there ever be, it shall only exist to bestow awe for the dubious of mind.

In truth, we are the wardens sitting in midst of our own prison cells while holding the very key to freedom and a doorway to remembrance.

The dream is yours, and, only by casting doubt aside, shall succeed to bring two worlds closer together.

"Into the dreamer's hand, all things become possible in a dream."

INFINITY

The purest abstraction of infinity is that which is limitless; capable of movement in all directions and endless facets regardless of color, formula, or shades of light.

Where infinity goes, numbers follow and should there ever be any hint of limits, none shall witness it.

Infinity is absolute, holding allegiance to nothing yet holding everything.

It stands upright and limp, it is smooth and coarse, it is a she and he or both and neither.

PETEH

So diverse is this word that nothing can diminish the truth of its nature, for infinity bears the likeness of a sphere, a central point where nothing touches all things.

"Infinity touches where we have yet to reach."

AAGAN

An adversary is the reflection of a tyrant, moving to coin the façade of respect; but justice wages war against the soldier of hubris, to end the machine of ego and pride with the law of truth whose business shares wealth through honesty.

Act 3

ADVERSARY

To the adversary, the kingdom of mammon - we're on to you.

We know what you do and how busy you have been.

What are you stirring with endless wealth from corners of the measured depths, seated upon a throne of darkness crowned in death?

Indeed, you may be subtle, but there is nothing holy in your works....... The mechanical wonders crafted to spoil you, the fiction spread to conceal you, and souls seduced to worship you - these are no more than finite fractions watched from above.

Behold, your wealth is shattered by your own scepter, and the Ancient of days shall consume all to create a new thing, where achievements wield no ego and death is the dust of ashes.

A greater will is at work to refine our future, with faith growing to crucify your fear a thousand fold.

All your wonders, your devices, and your evil shall be undone, filling the void your greed has stolen.

You are in for one miraculous ride amongst the best seats in all creation, *will you not join us for eternity?*

"In wisdom, the adversary's face is known."

REFLECTION

Our reflection tells much when it concerns us, outside those moments when we mask ourselves to engage today's kingdom; when we have no one to impress but ourselves in the silence of solitude.

It is then by which our face is recognized for what it is and not for the mask in its place.

Gaze into the mirror and foresee, who you are and what could be, for beyond life's menagerie is a face worn and tired, grieved and stressed.

What do you perceive in that moment, fears of life, doubts of success, or unhealthy dispositions with no way out?

Behold, within the reflection is the opposite; our opposition against us, thus making this key golden.

If there is anything you see that you do not like; rise and do something about it for better.

Opposition will not leave on its own; only by conscious choice to act will opposition submit into our favor.

Such amazing power we have at our hand, and our reflection serves to remind us of what we can do to overcome all enmity.

"A reflection is worth countless refinements."

TYRANT

Before the end of days, a generation of kings may rise to openly war against what was made good from the beginning.

If this becomes so, worry not for every action cannot stop the fulfillment of peace.

Consider the difference between kings ruled with peace in their souls from the tyrant who, behind peace, flatters many to destroy for servitude.

In cruelty, the latter shall assume the veil of peacemakers, but their works shall dethrone wise counsel.

No matter the cost, follow not one of these, for it is far better to defy their commands in peace than live with the guilt of stained hands as there never was, nor ever shall be such a thing as "honorable" evil.

Only the grief of torment is beneath the weight of a tyrant's grip and, if commanded to do evil in those days, then command it back to them to do it themselves and lift not a finger to aid in their own folly.

"A tyrant to others shall you become should you fulfill the will of a tyrant."

COIN

The coin rules over all flesh and bears no record in the spirit.

Today, there is no escaping the reality of the coin's seduction to be a necessary vice.

It's a reward for services rendered, granting access to a wider selection of choices which open opportunities to the finer comforts of living - food, drink, shelter, and entertainment.

Thus the coin grants privilege for anyone who has more over anyone who has less.

This principle is the bane that lures earthly kingdoms to race in war to covet the most coin for, whoever covets the most, shall establish the rule and declaration to secure their dominion over generations to come at the expense of the lesser's well being.

Such is the will of greed, and greed ensures the fall of even the mightiest kingdoms for greed causes tyranny to act above fairness.

Since the coin's glamour signaled the fall of kingdoms before by this very reason, the coin's luster remains to be translated and minted anew, only to begin once again.

And yet while the coin drives today's kingdom with a new mint, the fact of history repeating itself is pushed into obscurity and the chance to learn the spirit of error for all time is nearly forgotten until it's too late.

"In separation from spirit, the coin survives the times."

FAÇADE

Earthly kingdoms are like a façade, where its subjects awake to dress in legal attire, interact to exchange thoughts in moderated conduct, and are compelled by ritual to take part in the various roles the roulette of life has given.

We are seduced to see only the "light" within ourselves while ignoring the darker origins of our motives - a side that kindles the underbelly with a vague existence.

If truth be known, we unknowingly divide against ourselves, within a darkness held in check from cascading, through desire for earthly delights.

Lust is pushed above love, greed is admired beyond need, adoration for bloodshed is applauded, and secrecy to betray and overthow develops without concern.

Thus reality taints the façade and the sting of dismay is felt, yet here is a key to consider.

This is not a physical struggle, it is a spiritual one where souls are pressed heavily by a serpent's touch whose mockery has blackened throughout the years.

Understand, and the façade fades away, for the serpent's bane was never ours to begin.

"To see only the façade is to know a half life."

RESPECT

Actions are weighed and respect is earned, for the self to inspire the many.

Respect is a quality of appreciation for all things inspired, it stands firm as a standard to appreciate; in thought, motive, speech, and accountability.

To command respect of a people is to elevate one's own measure of self-worth, beyond fullness and without price, to defend the virtue of equity.

Anyone who works to absorb and practice this principle, earnestly, becomes a special kind of person, released from evil's grip and refined like pure gold.

What is learned here will not go unrewarded, for admiration shall be returned gratefully from surprised expressions of many, when something loosely applied is redeemed and brought forth fully as a golden spark to our era.

"Respect your worth to serve many."

JUSTICE

Dishonesty can never undermine justice, for justice sees truth as the light of day vanquishing the deceit of lies.

Justice upholds the equity of our civil and fundamental rights, where laws established would assist to carry the stability of welfare for people of all ages, creeds, and genders

Security of justice is not for the exclusive pleasure by they, who enjoy bending honest practice for their own leisure, neither is justice for anyone high or low to abuse for personal glory.

Justice is rights of impartiality; it's the very heart that separates fairness from abuse on both the lawgivers and the lawful.

There never can be a moment where justice can act without checks and balances, for even in the span of seconds, justice can slide to corruptive vileness if we act not to safeguard its measure, regardless of class.

"In the hand of righteousness is justice blessed."

WAR

A time is coming in which all earthly kingdoms that profit in war are reluctant to face.

War is ending beneath the touch of a divine hand.

Know and understand that the Ancient of days is before any kingdom, and now moves perfectly to reach many with a key that supplants literature, media, and propaganda.

The message is a timeless one……. *Peace.*

Peace, a lasting peace, greatly desired, shall overspread to reign freely, fine tuning willing souls to stand upright in heavenly splendor to ease the tender heart for all who see the horrific ugliness of war.

It is with hope that these words are written in earnest; watch for a people who shine bright with unbroken faith from heaven above, for their time is but a new beginning as the utopia of our fondest dreams brought forth.

"Leave war behind and know the promise of peace fulfilled."

SOLDIER

At ease, soldier.

Let comfort enter your hearts as these words are known; whether small or great, you matter.

It is too easy a thing to hate that which is not understood, more-so easier to pin blame on something else just to ease personal grief.

But, beyond social dogma, there is importance to what you do for the sake of security from the kingdom by which you have sworn to defend, even if it means death.

Indeed, one can only dare to imagine the burdens you bear, the despair, the sorrow of whatever it takes to fulfill orders given; but never let the weights swallow you, for you matter still.

Take notice and forever remember that you are not a number, nor a tag, neither someone in abject servitude; you are valued greatly for without you, the machine quakes to collapse and kings are rendered powerless under the heel of your boot.

Marvel not at this, for these words echo through time.

You are a soldier, defender of righteousness, protector of peace, and keeper of justice for all after you.

Now rise to face the day with new vigor and fulfill your oaths to king and country.

"Knight or soldier, neither is expendable."

HUBRIS

We are created with a greater objective: walk in the spirit, and touch the heavenly wisdom for each soul born to live.

To deviate from this is dreaded.

Thus be warned of hubris, the act of seizing spiritual thrones to distort the perfection of creation's plan.

Hubris, simply put, is excessive pride, even to the face of the beginning where perfect truth resides.

There is no mystery here, only reflection....... We are created beings, and no matter what we do, how we think, or the achievements we marveled to make throughout the generations, there will always be intelligence older and wiser than ourselves.

We can only delve to understand, for we are created and, in the greater scope of creation, we are young.

Notice how many earthly kingdoms before us were eager to assume this position of exultation before overcoming hubris, and notice how many before us were cast down by their wild boast into the pit of scornful vipers?

More than once, and more to be merely coincidence.

"With hubris, who can hope to last?"

MACHINE

The existence of the machine is greatly relied on for luxury's sake, where excellence, perfection, and speed for products and services rendered is timed to inhuman levels of precision.

There is nothing wrong with the machine's ambition to assist, however on the condition that the machine is never allowed to usurp the skill of a people.

When that happens, skill is lost, and fine craftsmanship within that kingdom shall erode to crumble on itself, ultimately to the point of the machine surpassing to replace personal development of creative works.

Take heed, and only excel the machine to assist in the joy of learning.

Never let any machine take the place of a people.

"A machine is best kept an extension of our will."

EGO

Ego is enemy to all.

It stands like a lowly gate made of selfish whims, for its solemn vow is to swear fealty to no one while proudly imposing its own might to every corner of its reach; leaving a noxious trail of desolate depravity.

Ego is self-serving, quick to grow where least expected, while holding a terrible defiance if identified in earnest to be removed.

There is no joy to be in ego's company, no pleasure in its motive.

Ego loves to hate as much as it hates to love, and is imagined to be the most loathsome of adversaries amongst wise counsel.

And for all conclusions reached, it is most likely so and true to heart, for anyone who encounters ego, prepare thyself well as the guarantee of blood shall surely be spilt from gashes made by ego's lust to divide, and destroy.

"A friendship with ego is the road to nowhere."

PRIDE

Pride is a luxury no one can afford.

The price of pride is far more than its worth and upon acceptance of this loan, the cost to repay is compounded with a merciless river of growing interest.

All of us are guilty to accept the allure of pride at some point in life, and many amongst us are paying back heavily for those fleeting moments of luxury; a regretful mistake, a missed opportunity, or perhaps a loss of loved ones are few of its recoils.

But know that the glory of pride constricts with a grip of bitterness.

There is no beauty in such, no lasting pleasures, and the only gift it has to offer is a golden cup filled with emptiness.

It is fruitful when pride's allure is rejected before it begins, and action without pride is worth far more than all the riches of the earth.

"Fascinations for pride are best left untouched."

LAW

A rightful entitlement to an upright standard of law, in fairness of equity is fundamental for people of all ages, creeds, and genders across the whole earth.

Anything less is uncivilized.

Amongst them is the freedom to prosper, the freedom to trade, the freedom to vote, the freedom to travel without bondage, and the freedom to defend the common good against all forms of tyranny.

This is not a law that any land can claim right to, nor can any kingdom claim ownership of, for this is a measure that is free for all with the aim of refining an inspired people of today to face future times greater than our own.

Peace, without evil to live well, without strife for youth and elder alike, and without greed, is the will this law gives with care.

This may stand merely as a dream today, but its vision will surely move into reality tomorrow by they who remember this testament.

"Only keep the law that provides with care."

TRUTH

There is no greater vice than to carry the burden of lies, a guilt that weighs heavily on the soul like an angst that cuts mercilessly into the heart.

If anyone tells you that lying is easy, then it is they who lie within themselves.

It is fair to say that people live to seek truth, and to receive and speak truth is perhaps as easy as the current of the purest waters flowing downstream to the most abundant seas abroad.

A lie, by comparison, stands as a block of filth that impedes the current, for one lie is required to cover another, and more is required to cover the first.

It is an endless craft of unethical creativity that, if one piece crumbles, all crumbles with the filth washing away, for truth ultimately emerges triumphantly.

Why subject yourself to hardship when it clearly benefits you to speak the plain truth concerning all matters?

It is a glorious feeling, and all who deal with you shall respect you dearly for all the words spoken forth from your lips.

"In all matters, defend truth."

BUSINESS

The practice of business establishes a social order within any earthly kingdom, to stabilize commerce, to promote trade, and to preserve general welfare from the remote times of our past to the cosmopolitans of today.

It stands as necessity, not luxury, if anything is to get done to ensure continued prosperity in the fairness of living.

We have grown accustomed to appreciate business.

However, there exists seven plagues that can subtly undo what is necessary within any business, so be warned to fervently destroy the following: deceit, deviousness, dishonesty, elitism, favoritism, greed, and injustice.

For any business motive to succeed, productivity is prosperous, only when honesty sets the key example with truth following close behind.

Anything less will tarnish a business into that which is evil and from evil, dust, bringing abject misery and ruin when least expected.

"Good business is honest and true."

WEALTH

It is preached that the love of money is the root of all evil.

And because of this, it is an easy thing to condemn all manner of wealth; however, take notice that wealth in itself is not evil, but allowing personal greed to covet more than is needed, is.

An excess of wealth, with the desire for yet more, only gives strength to an adversary who wars against all that is good.

Wealth acquired honestly and distributed to promote one's personal welfare need not be frowned upon, for this opens opportunity, not only for one's self, but equally so for those loved and the successors of new generations.

Taken with wisdom, the pursuit of wealth becomes a one-way door of opportunity that bestows finer rewards when entered.

But should that trust be broken by a shameless greed to covet, a wrench is cast into an otherwise perfect formula, which in turn encourages discord until the wrench is removed by choice.

"A land of wealth requires only what is needed."

HONESTY

A fantasy of intimacy inspires our youth of recent days, yet its reality is strangely absent until experience compels truth into a potentially painful awareness.

Such an ignorance can yield emotional strife, discord, and ultimately, desolation.

Thus a lasting intimacy has but one guiding principle - *honesty*.

Without honesty, there is nothing but shackles of iron, for honesty is a trusted wellspring where love resides; a wonder that never has to feel sorry, never has anything to conceal, and never betrays for a morsel of dust.

More importantly, it is by this guiding principle that can hope to promise a happier life between lovers of past, present, and times not yet foreseen.

Remember this always, and desolation can be happily forgotten.

"That which honesty holds never fades."

AHWEI

An artist who is unique may be an actor or the singer who can dance, take criticism, and have fun.

Act 4

ARTIST

The role of an artist has a key objective, to bring into existence an inspiration that has not yet been introduced, thus pioneering originality to encourage many generations.

It is not the role for any artist to mimic existing ideas, but to push into the envelope of the undiscovered and convey that language into a medium for all to experience.

If anyone were to observe an artist's work, then say in earnest, *cliché*, then that artist has deviated from the objective.

In truth, an artist is tuned to cross the bridge into a place some consider as imagination, while others reflect as chaos, yet it is the source where fresh, raw, and original thoughts flourish.

But if *cliché* becomes a ruling power, then an artist's work slips away to become lost in veils of vanity.

We hold this great marvel, to bring abstraction into coherence, originality into creativity.

It begins with thought and only an artist can shape it.

"An artist shapes creativity from originality."

UNIQUE

We are all unique.

Whether born by love or circumstance, the qualities inherent within each person are rarely, if ever, identical.

More importantly, let it be wholly understood that mental or physical challenges are only worth as much for documentation and nothing more.

It is in error to pity anyone, for people, from their time of birth, are given a birthright to live in goodness by that, which they are given to excel greatly at.

Each of us has strength and weakness, and the better part of life is to encourage strength while nurturing weakness, thus allowing both to heal together.

When the unique is accepted sincerely, from the special to the brilliant, only then can earthly kingdoms take the first true steps toward a humane credence for all its subjects.

"Unique is unique to no one."

ACTOR

Let us turn to appreciate the role of an actor, not for the glory the actor may receive from an audience, nor for the subjective nature of words brought forth from the actor's part.

None of it means anything towards what the actor is, from what the actor is not.

Here is an actor on stage, dressed in full character, before an audience whose presence means little, except one for all.

Here is an actor of style, as lines echo in crisp clarity, recited once, without blemish, at the level of poetry.

AHWEI

Here is an actor, with sights rising, leaving nothing, and giving beyond for the rapture of expression.

Here is an actor, poised with elegance without measure; for the actor knows that adoration is given by they who receive the actor's pleasantries, with glimmers of promise of what they imagine themselves to be; and yet, so few take actual steps to attain what the actor does by play of action.

We must appreciate their role in our lives, for without their inspiration, earthly kingdoms would be lost to crowns of stagnation.

"Flamboyance without fault is the aim of an actor."

SINGER

The passion of a singer's voice reaches into the depths of kindred souls and uplifts spirits out of troubled times and, through the singer's poetry, a vision sparks.

In pleasant lands we sit together in kinship; all woes are left behind; what is needless is cast aside.

A dream of a circle, around a cheery fire upon an emerald hill surrounded by waves of oceans, pure and free, becomes a clear sight.

There minstrels play and there we sit in peace upon the untouched stones, eager to feel the singer's melody that speaks of wondrous tales, and as the voice uplifts, so do we join in rhythmic subtle accord while absorbing words, echoed beneath the starlit sky.

AHWEI

Our lasting unity halts the burden of hardships and, as we gaze into each other, we understand one another without searching, for in that precious moment, we sing with the singer as one voice on one land, renewed by the vigor of our dreams released to overcome all trials.

"The majesty of a singer can bring many worlds together."

DANCE

Who told you, *you cannot dance?*

There is majesty in the beat, and the essence of dance is held close by a multitude of people from all creeds and genders.

Since the days of old, dance expresses its joy to release the downtrodden from sorrow and stress.

If truth be known, then dance is a language without words that speaks rhythmically between cultures.

And, as a dancer, it is one's ability to move within the vast sea of energy where its ripples overflow with sparkles of electric poetry.

In motion, energy vibrates and, from vibration, sound is felt and, from sound, colors burst in sheer brilliance within and roundabout for all bodies to enjoy.

> *"In dance, we move forward - in shyness, we hold back."*

CRITICISM

There are two types of criticism; both meanings subtly oppose each other and are not easy to distinguish, but once realized, wisdom separates wheat from chaff.

It is a fair observation to say that criticism for anything is not easily welcomed, especially for projects that take effort, thought, and time.

However, the criticism is not to blame; rather, it is in how the criticism is executed and received, for one type of criticism is constructive while its opposite scorns - *the judgement of one's merits vs. the disapproval of one's faults.*

These days, criticism is spoken with little regard to distinguish the two meanings and, when disapprovals without merit begin, creativity is struck down and the individual criticized is struck down.

Criticism is not about having bias against anyone; criticism is about enriching the progression of an idea to refine its development through constructive analysis - what can be done to make it better is the complete sum of criticism, and anything of negativity is unproductive and a waste of everyone's time.

"Aim for criticism by not blasting ideas conveyed."

FUN

Has your heart become so lifeless and cold that you have forgotten what it's like to have fun?

There is a difference between being responsible and having fun with your life and living responsibly without fun; the latter of which would be better if one's heart were beating inside a marble tomb, at the dead of winter, with no hope for escape.

Life without fun is life without care for one's well-being of the self.

It is not our nature to ignore the obvious, and, to care, is a quality that elevates awareness from instinct.

Fun is the synthesis of work and play, bringing elder and youth together to celebrate and share new moments of joy.

Where fun exists, opposition does not.

What does it matter who wins or loses when fun is around; who can resent when fun is placed first above assumptions?

Without a healthy balance of fun, life is absent and stagnant as second class beneath the rigor of labor; participation becomes forced, the experience empty, and life becomes irresponsibly dull.

"Go where the fun fully experiences the joys of life."

NAAMI

The tradition of death and darkness creates a paradox, a fable of wrath and religion, whose fate is the science of faith.

Act 5

TRADITION

Tradition is valid when teachings, passed between generations, assist in the growth of our youth, to succeed the elders before them to a state better than before.

But if tradition exists to oppose learning, then that tradition is best discarded and abandoned.

Great are the expectations of tradition, but less attention is given to the priority of what should and should not be passed.

We are known for being subjective, which is greatly amplified in our youth.

Yet the young are equally curious, like new sponges, absorbing every experience around them and integrating lessons learned into the fabric of their lives.

This molds them into the adults they shall become and, if used sincerely, tradition can elevate development to profound levels.

But if tradition, mixed with dross, is used against our youth, then growth becomes stunted for each generation, ensuring crumbled clones who war gloriously against fresh ideas.

"Keep every tradition by purging the dross."

DEATH

Death is like an elusive mistress that cannot be unclothed or tamed into subjection by earthly means.

Fear and dread faithfully follow death's footprints, garnished with a fascination and mystery alongside the question hotly debated amongst many - *what is beyond death?*

This can be a haunting question and, though many people are reluctant to admit it, death indeed weighs heavily, for a denial of life ultimately leads to death's embrace.

There are some who declare that there is nothing thereafter, a void of abject nothingness, while others contend that souls reincarnate through a wheel of karma.

But by their own reasoning, who is counted right amongst any of them, when death acts like a wild card shuffled, always shifting like that of the most forgotten of dreams?

"Death is life's mystery without end."

DARKNESS

In darkness, there is an allure so seductive that its very presence attracts willing souls to explore an array of pleasures lost to oblivion.

Many desire to embrace darkness eagerly without caring about the reality of its nature; and if wisdom is offered yet declined by their own hand, then let them be, for a test of trials is in their calling.

Keep in mind, that to perceive the fullness of knowledge may first deliver one to endure the deepest darkness before truly accepting the fate of what darkness holds.

More importantly, know the difference between darkness and evil, as evil is forever beneath darkness, and all subjects are given into their hand the choice to embrace darkness or light, fulfilling the destiny of creation.

As darkness moves to empower living souls to endure a journey of trials, evil is like a loathsome curse that seeks to conceal the knowledge of choice.

Remember this well - darkness serves like a necessity for creation's plan, a key that can only be reconciled through a cleared sight.

"The acceptance of darkness is light's mercy."

PARADOX

That, which has happened, makes the paradox impossible.

The flow of time past cannot be moved, altered or changed without a backlash of unpredictable consequence.

If anyone, by chance, succeeds to move backwards in time, then it was already meant to happen.

And if anyone desires to alter the flow of time for their own ends, then actions change nothing and time continues undisturbed, for every action taken moves perfectly with the flow of time.

This is how paradox works, ruling, unchallenged, to safeguard the past, like the still frames of a film being played for our amusement.

Once a still is captured in the present, that moment becomes locked unedited in the past, for the present is built from the past.

"Where time is bent, paradox straightens."

FABLE

Whenever earthly kingdoms suffer hardship, the desire to escape grows and the mind is lured to the fable, a tale of fantasy crafted to comfort the soul from life at their time.

This word, unfortunately, is seldom recognized over its modern counterpart, entertainment; designed to deviate by scattering attention to alternate times and places.

But the fable is the origin, holding a foreshadowing of ill tidings for anyone giving themselves wholly to the fable's service.

In truth, there is nothing wrong with the fable so long as its use teaches to dream of a greater sense for the life we are born to live.

However, if life is troubled and despair seeks to lose itself within the fable to avoid the worries of life, then a soul becomes a prisoner and a group of souls lost together are overthrown.

To what hope, then, is there for any kingdom if the fable is overindulged when it is neither the proper time nor place?

To perceive this distinction is key, for the worship of any fable to avoid life will, in the end, only yield withered fruit.

"The fable is a snare only to they who gladly live by nothing else."

WRATH

Wrath is a tempest of spite, an emotional fury, which loves to inflict anguish with little desire for regret.

The feeling of wrath is enjoyed best in the company of they who feel accused, cursed, grieved, outcast, slandered, tormented, or trapped and it stands as a defensive measure for release of tension, fiercely built up from within to its peak.

When at peace with a conscious heart, wrath becomes a mythology where even the mentioning of the word would be looked upon with scrutiny - *does wrath actually exist?*

Yet when wrath is actually unleashed to its full, the very act can scatter loved ones and smite the ground with vile revulsion.

It is neither pleasant, nor kind and only foolishness can dare to provoke wrath and hope to restore all that was lost in the aftermath.

"In wrath, everyone wins the grand prize of loss."

RELIGION

Many are unaware of what religion actually is from what it is not.

The kingdoms of the earth hold religion as a powerful order of influence and that agenda has lasted, nearly unchecked, for centuries.

There is nothing wrong with religion on its own, for religion holds the worship of faith to revere the spirit of heaven above.

But know that religion, that lies in bed with evil, does not go unnoticed and is watched from above, and there is a key difference between religion and religion that exercises rule over many at the expense of faith.

The appearance of earthbound benevolence does nothing but cast fractured traditions to stumble the way of faith in exchange for coin, favor, and servitude.

Truly, the faithful are brethren while deception is dross.

Know this distinction, and all is not lost.

"The keys of religion are yours to decide."

FATE

Fate and destiny go hand in hand and, like providence, there are many of the earth who feel they are meant for something more than what they are.

How little do we exercise our fate since fate defines destiny; always looking elsewhere except, where it counts the most, within ourselves.

Indeed, fate is strengthened when we truly believe in ourselves, and fate is granted only when belief in one's own dream is certain.

Effort is taken in thought, and from thought into action and in turn, divinity blesses that fate further into destiny.

We live by what we dream from our own thoughts and actions, then focus our destiny from what we believe into a tangible reality.

There is no mystery concerning fate except its lack of knowing; and only by accepting your own mastery, will greater dreams be possible with no end in sight.

"A dream believed is the fate of a brighter destiny."

SCIENCE

Where today's science is concerned, there is much to be said.

Science forgets what science is, in exchange for the glamour of comforts that science provides.

More importantly, today's science has favored itself to serve the funding of industry over the freedom of unbiased discovery.

Science is a useful tool, a valued asset given to increase awareness.

It is neither mysterious nor elusive.

And yet, science cannot be praised for claiming any absolute, for all ideas await to be tested, with new theories rewriting old theories.

Only the logic science provides is free for anyone to behold the why of how life on earth works.

This is the heart of the matter.

Individuals charged to explore science, for answers within and without are best kept beyond earthly means.

"Science is never cut into stone."

FAITH

There are two styles of faith, one worth believing in and one not at all; one leads to salvation while one leads to temptation.

Faith can touch divinity, and yet faith can be perverted to ensnare many underfoot for one's worship of evil.

Faith can be holy, but faith can never be cruel; just be aware of which one is good from the one which is not.

Keep the two separate as the night is from the day.

For they who worship lucre are not spiritual, and in cruelty, shall seek to condemn openly all opposition for the boast of their own name, without tolerance, and without a glint of mercy.

Know the difference, as the first is kinder than all hypocrisy.

"Faith is where lucre shall never be."

LASAM

The unity of people brings a friendship of love and affection, for the gift of life, health, pet, child, water, and food strengthens the relationship of beauty with nature and peace, which fills out nostalgia for neighbor and family.

Act 6

UNITY

Since the creation of war, evil has done a sly job to viciously divide the unity of a faithful people; but evil grossly underestimates the extraordinary resilience of a people's faith throughout time.

By design, we live as keepers of unity, endlessly searching for kinship in others of like mind; and, when paths cross together in fellowship, networks cross and friendships are forged.

On a grander scale, desperation can band a people together by an ideal respected in troubled times, which, in itself, becomes a strength to be reckoned with.

No matter how much evil is waged to divide and conquer, a single act of righteousness can unite many as easily as heavenly rays of golden light.

We the people....... Three words together, on their own, hold an unspeakable sense of earthly power.

Do not let any stings of evil discourage, for a people, united for a righteous cause, can shake our world to its very core against any adversary.

"A people in unity cannot be undone."

PEOPLE

People are people.

There are many who are born to fade in and fade out, never to be seen hereafter.

People are from all walks of life, of unique sizes, shapes, ages, colors, creeds, and genders.

Some laugh, others cry, and some love while others despise.

People can be joyous, but their frustration can be inspirational.

Some rise to greatness, while others simply dream of greatness.

It is enough to theorize that people are divided equally, for the strength of one is the weakness of another, and what is abundant in one is desired by another.

So never be quick to judge people, for one can never foresee what people can teach.

"Without people, learning is diminished."

FRIENDSHIP

Friendship is built neither on a bed of roses, nor is friendship one-sided, seeing the mask of façades and the kaleidoscope of rainbows.

There exists a full spectrum to a friendship, including a practical side, a hardship side, and strife, where the meat of a lasting friendship is weighed and tempered.

Friendship is true on all fronts and will not be lost to discord, even through tough and trying times.

To call someone friend takes energy to yield a lot more, and bonds between friends are entwined like elegant braids of hair, almost matching that of family, and not something easily cast aside through a personal sense of selfishness.

If a friendship is lost forever, then it never was.

Take this to heart, a true friendship that endures, will seal any breach and heal all sorrows strengthening the friendship all the more.

"A friendship strengthens on tried foundations."

LOVE

Love, a feeling machines can never hope to understand, a truth that the tyrant will cower from, and a power that evil shall flee from.

Do you not know that love is a sacred treasure?

Whether yes or no, it is only a question of time, for its joy is spreading.

Let it be known that love is the entwining of affection without end, the surety that binds all things.

By love, all things are possible, by love, friendships last, by love, truth is honored, and by love, loneliness is lost.

"Love is the sacred treasure of a righteous people."

AFFECTION

A kingdom's subjects are a people drawn to earthly affection; though some may contend affliction.

Since birth, we are donned with flesh of the body, bound to its desire to instinctually know the warmth of another.

We marvel at its voracious appetite and cringe at its motive, as we are at times compelled to act against ourselves to sate its hunger.

Sometimes, misguidance governs the impulse so most are neither guiltless nor to blame.

The reward of affection is but a tease to the flesh.

Like surges laced with sensational pleasure, we are moved to experience what affection has to offer, perhaps for procreation, reassuring that loneliness is but a myth or kindling bliss within one's soul countering a trying life.

There is nothing is wrong with affection so long as the fine line of warmth is not crossed beyond sanctioned ventures.

"Affection is perfect in the sincerity of endearment."

GIFT

What is a gift?

Is there a reason to give one?

Is there a need to receive one?

Are times demanding to bring one?

Is it troubling to say, I don't need one?

In times golden, a gift holds a spontaneous act of kindness.

However, in recent times, expectation has replaced kindness.

What was once given in sincerity is now given out of obligation, forced.

Have we forgotten ourselves to the point where automation supplants feeling?

Pause to recollect that moment and restore the quality in the intent of a gift.

If you feel like a machine giving or receiving a gift, then you know the sting of emptiness within.

"A true gift is never ruled by force."

LIFE

Life is like a game played; learned by few, unknown to many, and ignored by the uncaring.

Many considerations have been noted to record what life means, but for all ideas brought forth, none have yet to yield reality.

We are all born to live on the earth for a time; a plan reveals what might be done to ensure success.

We crawl, grow, then walk.

We learn, play, then perceive.

We study, test, then work.

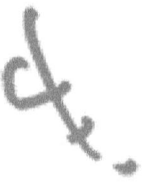

We buy, sell, then trade.

We plan, invest, then prosper.

We dream, pray, then create.

We hear, see, then wonder.

Near the end, when we reflect the past, we can raise a toast to honor any and all who live past wonder, for a heavenly life above all is the complete sum worthy of remembrance.

"If life is a game, then learn it well."

HEALTH

Health begins with a conscious awareness to learn the consequences of what unhealthy food has on a human body.

There exists a love hate relationship with health: to dream of the ideal physique while indulging in food that condemns the ideal to its own destruction.

Ask yourself, how can a living body thrive on food containing ingredients artificially created, catalogued with names both alarmingly long and unpronounceable?

Why is this grossly overlooked and ignored?

The body is created to reflect the heavenly splendor of holiness by healthy living, not to suffer what it cannot process.

Remember, a critical factor of healthy living is determined first by what is eaten.

There exists a solution without taking away one's desire for taste - be acutely attentive to all ingredients named.

If any ingredient is artificial, complicated, or blatantly unpronounceable, then be zealous to cast it away - this is the first step in reversing collateral damage, leading to a healthier you.

"Avoiding health is not without its price."

PET

A pet that is loved returns more love.

These curious creatures make remarkable companions, be it a dog, a cat, or perhaps a wild thing tamed.

Their loyalty is never questioned and we become their world as much as they become ours.

Few might see them as nothing more than animals, yet those who cherish a pet as their own are forever changed for the better, for they soon realize the difference between loneliness and friendship.

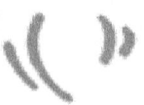

Though they may not speak in our language, theirs is unique, all its own, to be understood clearly when special bonds are formed.

May misery of regret strike swiftly into the soul of anyone who dares to inflict harm to any pet with malice, for their innocence holds little hardship and a pet's life beloved is key to what we, as neighbors, can do for each other.

"A pet adored eases the lonely heart."

CHILD

Our youth, a cherished treasure for all times, is worth more than a just measure of wealth, for all children born determine an earthly kingdom's future.

A child is like a blank canvas, willing to receive the best of wisdom made available, then shaped and molded by what is taught.

A child raised in love shall be loving.

A child raised in health shall be healthy.

A child raised in truth, shall be prosperous.

Remember well, a child cared for is neither a responsibility, nor a duty; but rather a blessing to receive and care, for they are the guarantee towards a lasting succession.

Be an inspiration to them so they can grow to be the inspiration for our future.

"To give better than what was given is reward sevenfold to a child."

WATER

The essence of water is our most precious resource on the earth.

Any healthy seed it touches kindles the cycles of life.

In its natural state, fresh water is clear to the sight and holds no taste, flowing freely in any direction it desires; it bears no shape except for that, which hopes to contain it.

Truly, water stands as the perfect cleanser to wash filth away, created by divine principle for the benefit of our well being; no elixir crafted by Man can ever hope to compare.

Priority is best given to the care and use of this precious resource, for which, without having, we cease to exist.

"Life is water, water is life - keep it pure."

FOOD

The joyful thorn of earthly kingdoms is a dependency on food while claiming there is never enough.

Did you not know there is already an abundance of nutritious food to feed the whole earth sevenfold?

Fruit, a commodity often overlooked, is a food blessed with seeds that can sow vast fields - *vast*....... Imagine the kingdoms of the earth and the hunger it suffers.

How much better would they be if all seeds planted were fruit trees and gardens that bore fruit to every home?

Consider, that each fruit grown yields more than one seed; with each seed planted and cared for, producing far more still.

Many subjects live only to perish from any number of circumstances; but to die from hunger, while neighbors relish abundance from the earth is cruelty.

No one need suffer this fate while seeds are readily available, and with wise usage of fruit, to grow and share symbiotically amongst neighbors, the scarceness of food would greatly diminish.

"A wealth of food begins with the seeds of fruit……."

RELATIONSHIP

The life search for a spouse has been the heart's desire for many subjects, whether it be from a personal need or guided by tradition.

Beyond the mask of appearances, however, gender is not relevant to this natural tendency.

The girls' allure yearns for the caring touch of romance, a lasting love for the safety to always feel enraptured.

Most boys look, but don't see beyond the allure of girls, for boys tend to first seek the ideal of their own fantasy, searching near and far, but never right before their eyes; regret is realized from the opportunity missed.

Can those, who are born to live the ways of both, be counted worthy to expeience the greatness of your mercies?

One might be surprised in the likeness between the genders, but here is a hope worth keeping; unless there is a faithful return to the expression of sincerest feelings held within, all locks and keys shall cease to fit perfectly.

"A relationship succeeds where hope is kindled."

BEAUTY

Has there been a time in which beauty was not misused?

In earthly kingdoms, since the days of ancient Egypt, techniques to exalt beauty hold a dilemma that continues to this day.

Ask yourself before your own reflection, *who can sincerely appreciate beauty for beauty's sake, without any expectations?*

Exalted beauty struggles against itself, for the worship of such techniques encourages expectations, thrusting the pure grace of beauty beneath the veil of a cracked mask.

Beauty exists, made perfect only for they who keep it, giving them full command over it.

LASAM

It shines like the sunlight and the stars illuminate it.

Eyes cannot depart from it, and yet it can stand with no need to change it.

From within, one's soul is where the best of us is weighed, and there is no earthly technique in all creation that could ever hope to match the radiance of beauty in the spirit of our souls.

This is beauty, when all appreciation is given graciously with interest, where beauty is cherished to truly stand on its own.

"All beauty requires, is you."

NATURE

Living perfectly in synthetic luxury is in direct opposition to living perfectly with wisdom that sustains nature.

If this isn't corrected, earthly kingdoms shall not endure.

Life is sustained by nature, and we are nourished because of nature, given as heavenly perfection, to provide for renewal of resources.

Nature flourishes throughout life, a vitality that exists within the plants sewn in the soil, within the whisper of trees, within the skies where the tempest of clouds wash the earth, and amongst the days that renew the seasons.

LASAM

However, synthetic thinking separates our connection to nature through the denial of its spiritual presence, because what is spiritual eludes science, and all earthly kingdoms are now fortified with this style of thinking.

Any earthly kingdom that thinks proudly of itself by wasting nature, shall not stand and no earthly kingdom has stood the test of time by this act.

When we return to live perfectly with nature nurturing more than what is wasted, only then can we receive the good blessings that can be accounted worthy even amongst the stars of heaven above.

"A return to nature renews life."

PEACE

Peace is being taken from the earth.

Let it be known that there are seven factors at work to prevent peace; seven factors that can be overcome through understanding.

For we are known to be many things, however evil is not amongst them since evil is beneath, seeking to encourage that peace be taken by the seduction of greed.

The greed for earthly power, for fame, for glamour, for land, for pleasures, for riches, and for servants, wars against peace, and so long as even one of these exists, peace shall never be.

Take heed for us all, for there shall come a time, when a people will band together in the spirit of everlasting peace.

Through peace, acts of love and empathy shall be blessed to return by the Ancient of days, to cast evil into a forgotten memory.

"The will to understand reveals the peace."

NOSTALGIA

Memories may be lost, but never forgotten, and all it takes is the right key to awaken what slumbers.

Nostalgia is like a sweet fragrance remembered, rekindling brief moments of innocence and pleasant things, of childhood dreams in simpler times long forgotten.

The right key will always trigger the right memory; a particular scent, a familiar taste, or something that catches the sight or brings music to the ears.

Once the trigger is released, we are suddenly transported, reflecting the best moments of that, which is brought to reflection.

It is a pleasant feeling unique to all who remember.

Should nostalgia be brought to awareness, savour the fullness of your moment, for as the memory fades, as one who is set free, time moves swiftly to fade nostalgia back into its hidden slumber.

"What was lost can always be nostalgia, even our memories."

NEIGHBOR

Do you fear the person next to you, behind you, in front of you, or perhaps afar from you?

Will it benefit you to pass judgement quickly over what you don't understand?

It is too common to easily condemn all the races for their faults, while placing their merits far away on the same level as strangers.

Nothing is further from the truth; together we share one earth, the same lands, the same seas, and the very air we breathe.

We share the same frequencies, the same molecules, including the finest particles yet to be discovered by science.

We are made simple from the beginning and have grown great to the end, and that journey has been shared to this day.

Though brethren by blood, even though we may not be family, it is uncharitable to think of anyone as less than neighbor, for the stranger is judged a debased person unworthy even to be civil with, and unless they themselves have richly earned condemnation, there is no need to supply it without surety.

Earthly kingdoms can bear a veil of darkness as easily as a cloak of light.

Who then is a stranger when so much is common amongst all people?

"Whether it be subject or king - each is a neighbor."

FAMILY

In all verity, family is all we have.

Consider, if one were to pause a moment to compare the number of kindred that are close, in direct relation to the number of people walking the earth, that number would be abjectly small.

Earthly kingdoms exist because of our social agreement to keep things ordered and our needs met.

It is natural for people around us each day to, at the very least, be civil to the point of being neighborly.

But what of family - intimate kinship by blood or feelings of love?

Both are rare but for some, not at all, bringing tearful sorrows.

Family is special, where even the ups and downs of the little things are not nearly as important as the bonds of support, companionship, and love the family brings.

There is warmth and strength when ties are close and a family's warmth should never be cast aside, for one can never guess when that warmth will fade away.

"Where family matters, there is much to be."

VONIS

Hands of freedom end duality through the cynic, whose lust for knowing transfiguration of sex, education, and ethics ignites the raw virtue of orient leadership, thereby growing to be the seer whose elder is sovereign.

Act 7

HANDS

There is something just that can be said about the artful success of achievements made by hands.

Imagine earthly kingdoms built inclusively by hands, where the machine is excluded fully from what our hands can create.

Would not its people gain the mastery of skilled craftsmanship from a life's dedication of practice?

Would it not yield a glory of creative satisfaction, one's empowered sense of renewal for self worth, without stagnation or apathy?

VONIS

Truly, to lose this key is dreaded.

So consider, should earthly kingdoms encourage personal craftsmanship, entrusting hands to be the sole appreciated vessel for skillful expression, a people's future would be assured to surpass where the machine cannot.

"By our hands shall expertise arise."

FREEDOM

Freedom is double-edged; on the upside there is no hindrance, no restraints, while the downside is limited only by luxuries coveted by evil intention.

The greater the luxury, the greater a chance for freedom to be traded or oppressed further into shackles of iron.

It's worth noting how easily freedom can be taken for granted and seized when held without valuing its loss.

All earthly kingdoms that have risen and fallen desired freedom.

Truly, wise sovereigns gave much for their subjects along with a timeless message passing from generation to generation - *remember*.......

After their time, what did it take to maintain freedom with the amount of cost, sacrifice, and tears shed for such an ideal?

If freedom is to be preserved in a changing world, then never forget to support its timeless defense against any and all oppression.

"None can dethrone freedom desired by many."

DUALITY

Good and evil, an instability that continues to confuse generations by pinning one against the other into a constant struggle.

However, there was once a time when everything was made good from the beginning, and then jealousy sewed its seed as an unwelcomed curse devoid of holiness.

A division was born, duality, that has crippled bloodlines to readily accept good and evil as equal to fit within traditions that earthly kingdoms crafted for their own benefit.

And yet, upon learning the origin of evil, who can now determine good from evil strictly by a king's royal decree?

It is not in duality that causes this oxymoron, but rather a preconceived notion to drink from a cup without first asking where the drink came from, thus fueling cycles of confusion between subjects of all ages.

We have only to see that our origin held no allegiance to duality since we are naturally drawn to rightly choose good over evil.

If evil was greater, then no kingdom could stand.

Consider this, and realize that duality is no more than an unwanted guest and like evil, both shall burn and perish at the end of time.

"Where duality resides, conflict follows."

CYNIC

Where self-interest rules over lies, the cynic observes that motive in exile with a curled upper lip.

It is no secret that greed is kindled by evil, fulfilling an age old dogma that inspires few to condemn many.

Many centuries have passed and many souls are needlessly lost for this selfish end, but nothing is what it seems.

Something precious, a free gift from the cosmos, is at work to evolve all aspects of social behavior.

Its promise passes through time like the finest gold.

It cannot be stopped, for the Ancient of days is timeless without measure.

So pay heed as the cynic is on to this: the ignored element of defiance against deceptions, a radical unmoved to conform while avoiding to fall through any of the traps laid solely for ignorance.

Thus unwelcome and key insight is held by the cynic, for nothing shall escape a cynic's notice to behold the reality of where we're from and where we're headed.

"The truth of a cynic is valued in a sea of lies."

LUST

There once was a Man who walked in the garden and was suddenly bit by the serpent's kiss.

The serpent's forked tongue hissed, *you are struck with lust - die with me.*

An anguish fell upon the man as he began to lose his way beyond the safety of the garden, to a harsher place filled with loathsome vipers.

There was no cure except time and as time passed, the euphoria faded and the man steadily returned, recalling who he once was.

It felt as a tempest like no other.

Awakening to a new vigor of clarity, the man vowed to reclaim what he lost.

A fiery sword appeared before him, and he took it.

Vipers slithered to block his way, but his fiery sword burned and the vipers fled.

When the man returned to the garden, his sword struck to pierce the serpent's kiss - *never again, it is you who shall be freed from me.*

The serpent's forked tongue hissed, *so be it, the garden is yours for you are worthy,* and the man walked past to the midst of the garden.

Vipers bowed before the Man in reverence, and the serpent crowned Him with seven eyes to see.

"*A wisdom in disguise is the kiss of lust.*"

TRANSFIGURATION

A time is near to fulfill an ancient promise, where a generation shall be blessed at the end of time.

In unity, a conscious people shall be changed, whose least among them shall surpass earthly kings and shall achieve what their elders did not.

Old kingdoms shall be undone and swept away by the strength of their love, neither by hatred, nor by cruelty, nor by evil, but by a faith so profound that its splendor shall appear as the Ancient of days, Creator of all things.

Wisdom shall leap forward from all walks of life to ways unimaginable from what existed before and evil shall burn away.

VONIS

Their hands shall rejoice to embrace the next level of life's journey freely, and its trigger shall be the dust from all that was once learned upon times built from itself.

Thus shall a divine people be freed forever to explore the heavenly wonders that await them in greeting, and peace shall wonder in joy.

"Transfiguration begins when the ancient is remembered."

SEX

The *exotic-erotic* thrill of sex is changed into a darkened industry, its gift of pleasure once honored is now muddled with mystery as the privation to wellness.

Doctrines decreed by earthly traditions dictate the joy of sex to be the gateway of all temptation, the core of deviation and any that cross beyond ecstasy shall pay the demanded payment, the fruit of new life expelled.

We are bullied to abhor while enticed to buy, sell, or trade the very act, whose reverence dwindles into traditions of profit, from one generation to the next.

By this course, the joy is driven away by cold words, love is cast down by fingers pointing with fearful scorn and more importantly, guilt is accused by self-righteousness, whose agenda divides righteous thinking.

From the moment of birth we are burned to adopt this life of sex without faith, and has anyone ever paused to see how severely we're being burned while we yet breathe?

"Where sex is honored, faithlessness cannot follow."

EDUCATION

A corruption that overspreads will first act with subtlety to restrict the richness of education taught to ensure its own rise to power.

Did you not know that corruption is in favor of a caste system of privilege, which tempts the educated to ensnare a lasting dominion over the uneducated?

Did you not know that education comes with a price, yet if coin becomes costly due to corruption, what will the fate of the uneducated be?

Consider, the greatest bane to any corruption, is when ordinary people gain the education to contend against spiritual bondage imposed upon them.

Thankfully, we are fortunate in our day to be blessed with powerful tools of education that the coin has not yet restricted.

So take the greatest advantage, do not deny yourself to learn what can be learned while education is readily available, of all studies that benefit to edify your own soul.

For all uneducated people make better slaves, and this is what corruption counts heavily on as the ace in its deck.

"Leverage comes only through education."

ETHICS

There once was a time, when people were compelled with the desire to defend the moral welfare of families and press such importance for their childrens' benefit.

The virtue of ethics was instructed early and passed between generations to preserve sovereignty from descending into the curse of evil.

This ideal, once appreciated and practiced diligently among families aspiring to nobler status, is becoming unappreciated and most times ignored with the advent of apathy.

But its importance has, if anything, emphasized a greater need to re-connect with ethics.

VONIS

Indeed, families forged in ethics shall live well, elevating their actions to understand the guiding principles of compassion, grace, justice, love, truth, sincerity, and wisdom.

To win the respect and admiration of all kingdoms, this key of understanding is like rediscovering a fountain whose waters are forever clear, clean, and pure - *who wouldn't like a taste?*

"A family rooted in ethics yields a rich reward."

RAW

A philosopher's tale of ancient's old, worth more than finer strands of gold.

Eat the raw living food and *live*.......

A healthy body will not live ideally if burned food is eaten exclusively, for a healthy body will not thrive from burned food, neither will an unhealthy body thrive from living food.

Raw living food separate from fire is the best of all required and shall restore excellent health if kept in faith of practice.

For the sick, sorrowful, and downtrodden, to eat in harmony with the raw principle, shall cause illness to diminish, bestowing life as once established by the Ancient of days.

"Raw living foods are boundless to good things."

VIRTUE

A person who swears fealty to virtue will neither be self-righteous nor selfish, and all their actions shall be modest and true to the hope of spreading inspiration.

Virtue is righteous, and a kingdom blessed can be measured by the quality of virtue between land, subject, and king.

It is what elevates consciousness into spiritual insight.

Daily cleansing, clean attire, healthy living, and sincere hunger for wisdom, transforms every virtue into pleasant creations and seizes fear to dissolve its legacy.

For there is no fear where none exists, and a virtuous people commits all to stand above mockery by aligning with this key.

Truly, virtue is like the catalyst of a new thing best applied not only to ourselves, but equally into all things created, to pave a smoother way for each generation.

"Inheritance is perfected when virtue is cherished."

ORIENT

The orient of our world is rich with a key unique to our time.

Much can be said to restore what this earthly kingdom once refined.

But one can only wonder if the peaceful of days old would be in agreement with their children living today.

To be static through violence was never the intent, but rather a spiritual life with teachings written in elegant script, with wisdom to uplift our youth, and with reverence to heal the soul as ideals to live by for generations.

Violence and peace do not share the same house nor eat the same bread, and understand that the orient's past is too precious to let evil supplant what has worked faithfully since the beginning.

There is no exception for violence to subvert divinity upon the earth, especially when the orient's purpose had been to prevent the descent to evil.

"The past of the orient is wealth for all seekers."

LEADERSHIP

To touch true leadership is to be like the sun of a midsummer's day, in times of peace or times of trouble.

Let it be known that the few, who stand upright to carry the banner of leadership, are nothing without the loyalty of a people swearing fealty of their promises to fulfill.

The caliber of leadership asks for nothing and gives everything for the sake of a given cause, a united voice empowered in faithful trust, for all to follow.

All shall appreciate and none shall question just leadership, and leaders who carry this quality are a sight to behold for their foundation is true, and faith can be placed on their shoulders.

Betrayal shall never leave their lips, neither in their thoughts nor in their actions. Fairness shall guide their steps, and lies shall flee from their actions.

However, a leader, who willfully breaks the oath of their leadership to a trusting people, falls as a betrayer and is best expelled swiftly, appointing their portion of influence to another worthy to fulfill.

"In leadership, fulfillment of promise yields no exception."

SEER

As keepers of unbroken truth, the seer beholds a vision.

The seer is the symbol of a messenger who is given a key to perceive what many have yet to.

The way of the seer is not so unique, but few are made between many generations to excel keenly in the youth, wiser in years.

They are often tried and tempered against all odds, yet are relied upon heavily in times of trouble, for they hold lost insight concerning records unkept.

Their journey is a thankless life, but one the seer is prepared to endure, regardless of the price paid against themselves for the wisdom held close within.

Where puzzles need missing pieces, it will be for the seer to reveal them, for their existence stands with power to reveal what is, but long since forgotten.

"The seer restores what kingdoms forget."

ELDER

It is an act of wisdom to show respect to all elders met.

They have lived on the earth longer, and it is right to honor them in fair judgement.

The youth is naturally fresh to experience, like a fiery blade to be forged in the crucible of life's journey.

Be comforted to seek the honest counsel of elders, for their tempered blades exist to offer experience; they are our fathers, mentors, mothers, and seniors, a cornerstone that holds the goodness of earthly kingdoms in remembrance.

Rebelliousness has no place to challenge wise counsel, nor is there any place to belittle goodly words from an elder.

VONIS

If anything, be civil in reverence.

Consider their past and the length of time by which they lived.

Their knowledge stems from the span of years, in their hope to prevent regret from repeating upon all who shall succeed their years.

If our youth shall learn a new thing, then it stands for them to realize that an elder's testament is something never to be taken lightly.

"Foundations are preserved by wisdom of an elder."

SOVEREIGN

Sovereign....... A word virtually unspoken of in today's language, a word slipped away into the tongue of forgetfulness.

But take note, that which has slumbered can now be rekindled, and that which was dormant can now be ignited.

The word, sovereign, carries with it the power of perfected praise.

Truly, each one of us is uniquely qualified to carry the quality of a sovereign; a firm reminder that, as a sovereign, we hold a solemn duty to forever inspire perfection for ourselves and each other into an excellence that forever shatters any limits that bind us.

Our growth is to excel above and beyond, not to wither beneath the weights and, to be a sovereign, encourages the driving force to surpass that priority.

So from this point forward, now and forever, let sovereign be acknowledged as a word of key importance and let it never be exclusive to the secret of few.

"Rise sovereign, and behold the fullness of your potential."

A Little Thought Book
88 Keys of Consciousness

Index

WORD	ACT # | KEY #	WORD	ACT # | KEY #
Actor	4 | 39	Elder	7 | 87
Adversary	3 | 19	Ethics	7 | 81
Affection	6 | 58	Fable	5 | 48
Artist	4 | 37	Façade	3 | 23
Atlantis	1 | 02	Faith	5 | 53
Beauty	6 | 67	Family	6 | 72
Business	3 | 34	Fate	5 | 51
Change	1 | 04	Food	6 | 65
Child	6 | 63	Freedom	7 | 74
Choice	1 | 03	Friendship	6 | 56
Coin	3 | 22	Fun	4 | 43
Conscious	2 | 08	Future	2 | 10
Creation	2 | 16	Gift	6 | 59
Criticism	4 | 42	Hands	7 | 73
Cynic	7 | 76	Health	6 | 61
Dance	4 | 41	Honesty	3 | 36
Darkness	5 | 46	Hubris	3 | 28
Death	5 | 45	Infinity	2 | 18
Dream	2 | 17	Insight	2 | 11
Duality	7 | 75	Justice	3 | 25
Education	7 | 80	Key	2 | 07
Ego	3 | 30	Kingdom	1 | 05

WORD	ACT #	KEY #	WORD	ACT #	KEY #
Law	3	32	Respect	3	24
Leadership	7	85	Science	5	52
Life	6	60	Seer	7	86
Love	6	57	Sex	7	79
Lust	7	77	Singer	4	40
Machine	3	29	Soldier	3	27
Magic	2	15	Sovereign	7	88
Message	1	01	Symbol	2	14
Nature	6	68	Time	2	13
Neighbor	6	71	Tradition	5	44
Network	2	12	Tranquility	2	09
Nostalgia	6	70	Transfiguration	7	78
Orient	7	84	Truth	3	33
Paradox	5	47	Tyrant	3	21
Peace	6	69	Unique	4	38
People	6	55	Unity	6	54
Pet	6	62	Virtue	7	83
Pride	3	31	War	3	26
Raw	7	82	Water	6	64
Reflection	3	20	Wealth	3	35
Relationship	6	66	World	1	06
Religion	5	50	Wrath	5	49

A Little Thought Book
88 Keys of Consciousness

About the Author

"It all begins with an idea......."

A question might be raised as to who the author of this work is. All that can be said is that the author is like you, moving through life, working earnestly to create a foundation that can allow future works to be conveyed through writing, visual media, and sound. For starters, my name is Al. Many people have I encountered along the way, of which without would not have made me into who I am today. All my life I held a talent for writing my thoughts, and in foolishness, I never realized the obvious until now. But once my talent was realized, words flowed, the imagination kindled, and a literary work was born to prosper for all to know.

In a kingdom of opportunities, I have given my all to pursue a vision. Perhaps you can relate? More-so, it is a dream for writing that keeps me focused in the game of life, to see what can be developed next in the years ahead. Truly, if you can relate to my words, then you will have taken a step further to know a bit more about me - as a writer, a neighbor, and perhaps a friend.

Al Rush

About Professional Misfits, Inc.

"Our thoughts to inspire......."

Professional Misfits, Inc. is a newly formed corporation established in Chicago, IL. Our area of focus lies in publication and we believe that the passage of wisdom can be successfully conveyed through writing, visual media, and sound. Our products are created to elevate consciousness and we aim to develop inspired ideas, encouraging inspiration into a medium that can be accessible by all. By challenging ourselves, Professional Misfits, Inc. will challenge many to behold the richness of their own souls. All dreams begin with a spark of inspiration, and our passion is to make the vision of our dream blossom into a golden reality.

www.professionalmisfits.com

www.ingramcontent.com/pod-product-compliance
Lightning Source LLC
Chambersburg PA
CBHW080450170426
43196CB00016B/2743